ELLA
Diaries

TOP
SECRET!

Meredith Costain

For Alexandra, Alicia, Annie, Aristea, Claire, Esther, Gen, Kitty, Lucy, Miette, Robert and Zac from Gold St PS Reading Club. Jingle all the way!—MC

Danielle McDonald

For Jade and Zoe, Jordan and Lauren, Jack, Katelyn and Alex.—DM

Scholastic Australia
345 Pacific Highway Lindfield NSW 2070
An imprint of Scholastic Australia Pty Limited
PO Box 579 Gosford NSW 2250
ABN 11 000 614 577
www.scholastic.com.au

Part of the Scholastic Group
Sydney • Auckland • New York • Toronto • London • Mexico City • New Delhi • Hong Kong • Buenos Aires • Puerto Rico

Published by Scholastic Australia in 2015.

National Library of Australia Cataloguing-in-Publication entry

Creator: Costain, Meredith, 1955- author.
Title: Christmas chaos / Meredith Costain; Danielle McDonald.
ISBN: 9781760153052 (paperback)
Series: Costain, Meredith, 1955- Ella diaries; 5.
Target Audience: For primary school age.
Subjects: Christmas stories.
Friendship--Juvenile fiction
Vacations--Juvenile fiction.
Other Creators/Contributors: McDonald, Danielle, illustrator.
Dewey Number: A823.3

ISBN: 978-93-5275-642-1

Typeset in Sweetie Pie.

This reprint edition January 2026

Printed in India at Shivam Offset Press, New Delhi

ELLA Diaries

Christmas CHAOS

Saturday afternoon

Dear Diary,

We've finally arrived at Moonlight Gardens, our home for the next two weeks. Yay! It is going to be fanTABulously fabulous.

Moonlight Gardens is a caravan park in Moonlight Bay, which is the best beach in the whole wild world. My family comes here every year for Christmas.

There are Good Things and Bad Things about staying in a caravan park.

Good Things	Bad Things
Caravans have cute little bunks and tables and chairs.	Caravans are **super squishy** and there's nowhere to put anything.
Every night is like a **giant sleepover** with your family.	You have to share a triple bunk bed with your little sister and brother. **Bleuchhh.**

Good Things	Bad Things
The beach is right next door!	The shower block is about 9 million light-years away. And if you aren't careful on the way there you might stand on a rusty bit of tin like Jimmy Pappas did. His foot swelled up like a balloon and turned black and nearly had to be cut off. Eww.

You get to eat yummy 'no mess' holiday food like Dad's 'surprise'* jaffles and mince pies and lots of takeaway meals.

EVERYONE sleeps in the same room so if you have Mexican takeaway for dinner and someone makes a bad smell there is NO ESCAPE. Double bleuchhh.

* We call Dad's jaffles this because you never know what's going to be in them.

Good Things	Bad Things
You can make new friends and you get to see them every year. 	You miss your friends from school. 
You can take your pets with you. Which means Bob is here too! 	There are other kinds of animals around that not everyone loves. Mainly SPIDERS. Sadly, my dad is an arachnophobe.** 

** Arachnophobes are people who start screaming and running around like maniacs if they see or even THINK about a spider or even a part of it, like one of its hairy, scary legs or giganterous fangs or googly eyes.

This year is extra-special because my BFF Zoe is going to be staying at Moonlight Gardens too! Her family is coming tomorrow and they are renting a caravan in the same row as ours. Yay!

We can go to the beach and the carnival

and the Christmas market

and eat crazy-flavour gelato.

And I can introduce her to Jessie and Ana, who are my SBFFs***, and we can do all kinds of magnificently marvellous holiday stuff together.

It is going to be excellent.

Bye for now. It's time to hit the beach!

Love, Ella

XOXO

*** SBFFs = Summer Best Friends Forever

Saturday night, just before lights out

Dearest Diary,

I kept looking out for Jessie and Ana the whole time we were at the beach, but they didn't show up. They probably haven't arrived yet.

Jessie is horse mad, just like Zoe. She wants to be a bareback-riding circus star when she grows up.

Ana loves drawing and painting.

Their families always come to Moonlight Gardens at Christmas time too and we do everything together, like cartwheels on the beach, and rock-pooling, and making mermaids out of sand.

And every year we do this special thing called the

Summer Wish

The rules go like this:

We have our first swim of the summer together, then make a wish.

If we do it exactly like that, our wish will absolutely, positively 100% for sure come true. But if we don't do our swim together, we will have bad luck to the power of 100 for the next year.

So I didn't go for a swim today, even though I really wanted to. I'm sure I'll see them tomorrow!

Good night!
Ella

Sunday night

Dear Diary,

Zoe is here! We had the best time today. I showed her ALL my favourite places.

First we went to the rock pools and pretended to be internationally famous marine scientists doing important research projects on the local sea creatures.

I love the rock pools. They're really special, because you can only go there when the tide is out. And there's this big cliff with little private caves, so I sometimes go there when I feel like being alone.

But it was fun to share my special place with Zoe. Here's what we saw:

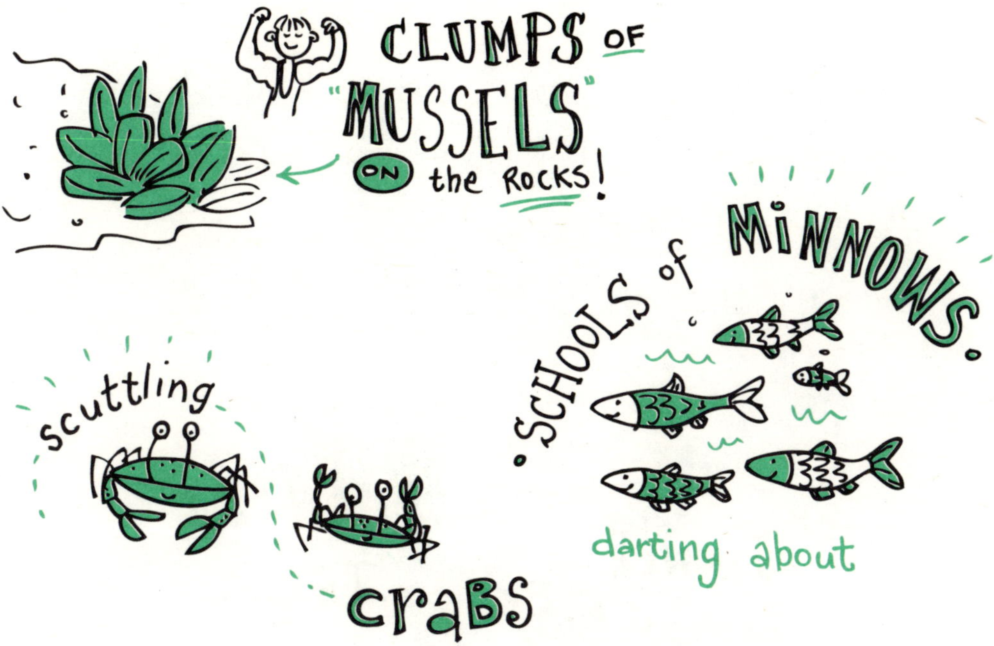

After all that important research we needed to ~~recooparate~~ ~~recorperate~~ cool down so we went for a nice refreshing swim in the sea. I wanted to wait for Jessie and Ana of course, so we could make our wish. But I STILL couldn't find them, so I went in anyway. I hope they'll understand.

Plus I have new bathers that I designed myself and I couldn't wait any longer to try them out. EVERYONE was looking at them, because they are SO SUPER STYLISH.

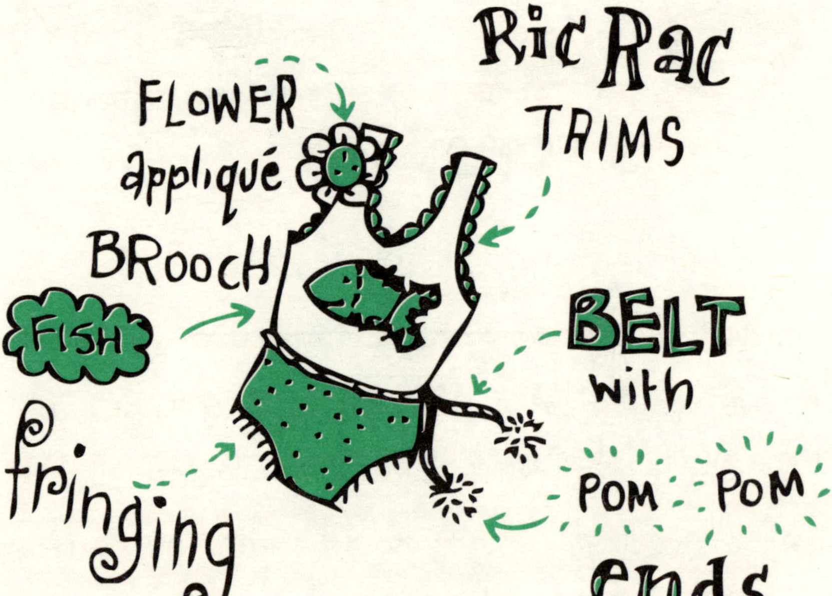

Zoe and I jumped around in the wavy waves, shrieking like seagulls. The tide was coming in and we got dumped THREE TIMES.

Next stop, the Gelato Shop! YUM!

Everything was magnificently marvellous. The sun shone shinily and the breeze breezed gently. It was the most perfectly perfect day in the entire history of perfect days.

And then something horrendous and horrifically horrible happened.

Well, we THINK it happened. We're still not 100% sure.

It was like this.

Mum and Dad took us all to the carnival. There were happy, smiling people everywhere, eating fairy floss and lining up for the rides. Of course, we all wanted to go on EVERYthing, but Dad said we could only choose one ride each.

Olivia was desperate to go on the Vomitrex but Mum said no way was she letting her go on something with a name that had the word VOMIT in it.

Even when Olivia said, 'Please, please, please, I am seriously desperate, I promise to keep my room tidy and help with the dishes forever and ever cross my heart hope to die!' (which she learned from me and usually works), Mum *still* wouldn't let her.

So then Olivia started having a little tanty, stamping her foot and blubbing like a big baby. EVERYONE was staring at her. It was soooo EMBARRASSING.

And then Mum said if she was going to act like a baby she had to go on a baby's ride.

So Olivia had to go with Max on the boring old Chair-O-Plane. It wasn't even a real one. Max didn't mind though. He likes everything.

Exciting REAL CHAIR-O-PLANE

BORING

Kiddy CHAIR-O-PLANE

But that wasn't the Horrendously Horrible Thing. The Horrendously Horrible Thing is so horrible I can't write about it right now.

I'll try and tell you tomorrow.

Good night, Diary.
Sweet dreams.
E x

Sunday night, really, really, really late

Dear Diary,

I've been lying here on my bunk **FOR HOURS** in **desperating despair**, trying to go to sleep.

REASONS I CAN'T GO TO SLEEP

1. There are scary animal noises coming from the scary trees outside our caravan.

2 My entire family (including Bob) is **snoring** like a bunch of **wallowing walruses** in a snoring competition.

3 I can't stop thinking about the **Horrendously Horrible Thing**.

So after about 900 hours of tossing and turning like a tiny boat being knocked about by giganterous towering waves, I gave up trying to get to sleep and climbed down TWO whole ladders so I could get Dad's keychain out of his coat pocket. It has this cool little pen light on it, which is why I can now see to write all this! ☺

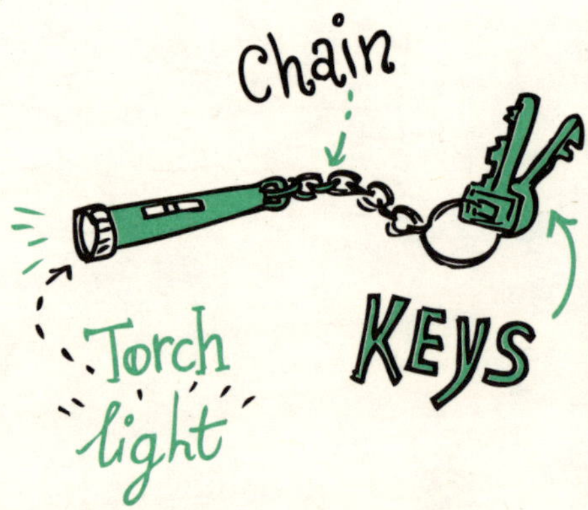

Uh-oh. I think someone just woke up.

Guess who?

Here's what we said to each other:

Olivia (in that whingey, whiny voice she always uses when she wants her own way): Ell-aaaa, turn the light out.

Me (whispering): Ssshhhh. You'll wake everyone up.

Olivia: You already did.

Me (still whispering): No I didn't. Go back to sleep.

Olivia: Make me.

Me (sighing): You are such a BABY, Olivia.

Olivia: I know where you got that light from. I am soooo telling on you.

And then Mum called out to tell us to stop arguing and go back to sleep or there would be Big Trouble.

So I waited for a bit, doing some fake snores so Mum would think I was asleep, and then I snuggled down really deep into my sleeping bag so no-one else could see the pen light and kept on writing.

Here's the Horrendously Horrible Thing that happened at the carnival today.

It was Zoe's and my turn to choose our rides. And of course we had to choose the same thing, because we are **BFFs**, and **BFFs** always do **EVERYTHING** together.*

* Sometimes Zoe and I even have the same thoughts or dreams at exactly the same time, which is **REALLY SPOOKY**. I am thinking of writing to one of those TV shows to tell them about it, in case they want to come to my house and make a ~~dock~~ documentary about ~~me~~ us.

Choosing our rides was taking forever because Zoe kept choosing things I didn't like (like the wobbly walk) and I kept choosing things *she* didn't like (like the Tip-O-Rama). And then Dad said everyone was getting bored of standing around waiting and if we didn't make our minds up in the next ten seconds he'd make both of us go on the Chair-O-Plane too.

NO WAY were we going on a BABY ride. What if someone saw us! Eww.

So we quickly chose the Ferris wheel. It wasn't as exciting as the Vomitrex but at least we could talk to each other without our brains **exploding** from watching everyone around us screaming and throwing up.

WHAT WE TALKED ABOUT ON THE FERRIS WHEEL

1. School

2. The people at school

3. How fanTABulously fabulous it is to be in a place for two whole weeks WITHOUT irritating and annoying people like Perfect Princess Peach Parker (the most exasperatering person in our class as well as the ENTIRE UNIVERSE) being annoying and irritating all the time and ruining our lives.

And then just as we were saying this last bit, **WE SAW HER!!! Peach**. In Moonlight Bay. **NO!!!**

Well, we *think* we saw her. We were **VERY** high up. And it might have just been someone who **LOOKS** like Peach.

And then I remembered our excellent teacher, Ms Weiss, who is exceptionally stylish (like me) and who knows a **LOT** of interesting facts (also like me) telling our class that:

7.29 billion is **A VERY BIG NUMBER**. So big it is **EXTREMELY** possible that two people out of all those millions and billions might look a bit like each other.

Yes. That must be it. That girl we saw at the carnival was just someone who **LOOKS** like Peach.

There is **absolutely, positively, definitely** nothing to worry about at all.

Phew. I can go to sleep now. For real.

Good night, dearest Diary.

Monday morning, really, really early, so early everyone else in the whole world is still asleep (unless they live in countries on the other side of it, where things like time are upside down)

Dear Diary,

I was in the middle of this amazing dream where I was being awarded the No Bell Fashion Prize for Excellence in Fashion Design when something tapped on my window.

I woke up and instantly went into **ninja attack** mode in case one of the scary animals had moved out of the scary trees and decided to set up a scary home in our caravan, and I needed to protect my weak and defenceless family from them.

But it wasn't a scary animal.

It was Zoe. In bunny rabbit PJs.

I stared out at her through the tiny window next to my bunk. 'What?' I mouthed.* Then I made a series of complicated hand signals to let Zoe know to be quiet because everyone else in my family was still asleep.

Zoe did some complicated hand signals of her own. Then she mouthed back, 'I need to talk to you urgently.'

* 'Mouthing' means opening and shutting your mouth so it looks like you're speaking when you are actually not. It is the kind of thing **Top-secret secret detectives** (and probably also ninjas) do all the time when they are on **Top-secret secret missions** and don't want anyone to hear the **Top-secret secret things** they are saying to each other.

I cunningly switched from **ninja attack mode** into **ninja stealth mode** and stealthily climbed down the bunk ladders, being extra careful not to wake any of the wallowing walruses (especially the large furry one).

'Why?' I said, when I was safely outside.

Zoe said she had been awake ALL NIGHT worrying that Peach had followed us all the way to Moonlight Bay so she could ruin our holiday and it was coming true already and we needed to have an Emergency Meeting** about it.

** Zoe and I always have Emergency Meetings when we have big problems to solve. Which is most of the time.

And I said don't be such a Panic Pants, we don't even know for sure the girl we saw *was* Peach. And then I told her my **fanTABulously fabulous** theory about the 7.29 billion people and she said: 'Stop it, Ella, it is too early in the morning for sums. **You are making my head explode!**'

Zoe's face looked like she'd been on the Vomitrex six times in a row without stopping, which made me feel really bad about calling her a Panic Pants. So I said: 'Oh, all right then, meet me at the shower block at Oh 900 hours.' (Which is the way Top-secret secret detectives speak when they are arranging their own Emergency Meeting times.) And then we both went back to our caravans and instantly fell into a deep, calming, relaxful sleep.***

*** The kind of sleep Sleeping Beauty had except ours only lasted for 15 minutes instead of 100 years, because a spider accidentally crawled across Dad's face and he ~~shreeked~~ ~~shreaked~~ screamed so loudly it woke up everyone in the whole caravan park. Including me and Zoe.

Have to go now, Diary.

CU soon!

E

xoxo

Monday night, just before lights out

Hey Diary,

Something really weird happened today. I was on my way to the shower block to meet Zoe at Oh 900 hours just like we arranged. And guess what?!

You never will because it is too weird so I'll just tell you.

I bumped into Jessie and Ana.

Our conversation went like this:

Me (excitered to see them): Hi, Jessie! Hi, Ana! When did you get here?

Jessie (not quite so excitered): Oh. Hi, Ella. Um, on Friday.

Me (puzzled and a bit hurt): Really?

Ana: Yeah. Sorry we haven't caught up yet but we've been kind of busy.

Jessie: Yeah.

Me: I looked for you at the beach yesterday.

Ana: Oh. Um. Well, actually, we didn't go to the beach. We went to the pool at that big new resort.

(Big new resort? What big new resort? And why didn't they ask me?)

Jessie: Yeah. We met this girl—she's really nice, isn't she, Ana?

Ana (nodding): And funny! She's so funny! You'd love her. And she has **REALLY** nice clothes. So anyway, she invited us to swim in her pool. You know, at the *resort*.

Jessie: You should see the pool! It's got all these beautiful gardens around it, with flowers and everything.

Ana: And palm trees.

Jessie: And water flowing out of a LION'S HEAD!

Ana: And you can lie around on special long chairs and a man brings you drinks with little umbrellas in them.

Jessie: It was just like being movie stars in a movie!

Ana: And guess what else?!

I didn't get a chance to guess what else because the time on my watch clicked over to Oh 900 hours and I suddenly remembered my Emergency Meeting with Zoe. So I said goodbye to Jessie and Ana and quickly jogged to the shower block where Zoe was waiting for me.

When I got there I told Zoe about my friends and the Mysterious Girl and missing out on our special swimming wish. And how I was now going to have bad luck for the whole of next year. Maybe for the whole of the rest of my life!

And Zoe said: 'It sounds like they don't want to be your friends anymore.'

And I said: 'So what, who cares? Who needs them anyway?'

And Zoe said: 'Never mind, Ella, we can do our own special swimming wish. Just you and me.'

And so we forgot all about our Emergency Meeting and went for a swim instead.

Good night
Sleep tight
Don't let
The spiders bite!

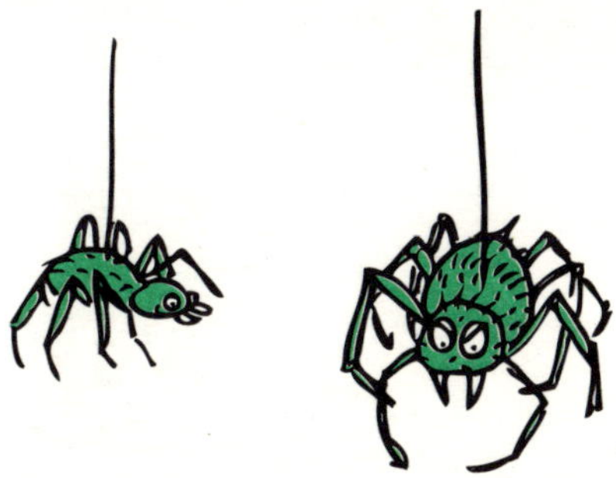

E x

Tuesday night

Hello Diary,

Zoe's mum took us to the Christmas market. It was aMAZing. Here's some of the Christmassy stuff we saw:

Mince
PIES
Kids
carolling
CAROLS
GingerBREAD
HOUSES
JAM
Pickles
Giganterous
CHRISTMAS tree

And then we saw this poster:

I CAN'T WAIT for Christmas Eve. And guess what? Zoe and I (and Bob) are going to enter the Pets and their Owners competition. We'll win for sure!

Wednesday night

Hey there, Diary,

Today was exceptionally excellent!

Zoe and I made a sand mermaid out of stuff we collected on the beach. And a lady came along and said it was the most beautifullest sand ~~sculpcher~~ sculpture she had ever seen.

And then she took a photo of it for the local paper.

We are going to be **Famous!!**

Love,
(Celebrity) Ella

Thursday night

Dear Diary,

Today has NOT been exceptionally excellent.

It rained. All day. WITHOUT STOPPING.

So we were stuck inside our caravan FOR THE WHOLE DAY doing boring family things, like playing charades and cards and board games that are so old they have dinosaur drool on them.

Even the spiders on the ceiling above Dad's bed (who were waiting for it to be night-time so they could drop down and play hide-and-seek in his new holiday beard—eww) looked bored.

Dad kept smiling at Mum and saying in a jolly voice, 'This is fun, isn't it, kids?' or, 'I'm SO glad it's raining, we never get to do lovely, fun family stuff like this all together!'

when he was probably ~~sek~~ secretly wishing it would stop raining so we would all go off to the beach for the day to ~~frollick~~ frolic in the waves and he could go fishing with his best mates, Wally and Davo.

I was just about to start climbing the walls when there was a knock on the door.

Everyone (~~including~~ especially Bob) looked at the door hopefully in case it was someone exciting like a pizza delivery person.

The Bad News

It wasn't. ☹

The Good News

It was Zoe. Yay!

We went out to our annexe so we could talk ~~privetly~~ privately without Olivia flapping her big ears and listening in. This is what we said:

Me (yawning): I am SO BORED.

Zoe (yawning back): Same.

Me: My dad is making my head explode.

Zoe: So is my mum.

Me (sighing resignedly): But what can we do about it? Everything is hopelessly hopeless.

Zoe (her eyes going all shiny like the star on the top of a Christmas tree): That's what I came to tell you. Mum and I went to the library to get some books so we didn't die deadifying deaths from being bored and guess what!

Me: There was an internationally famous movie director there who wants us to star in his next movie?

Zoe: Nope. Guess again.

Me: Cassi Valentine is being dropped into Moonlight Bay by helicopter to sing carols at the Christmas Eve concert and wants me to do a duet with her?

Zoe: Nope. Guess again.

Me: The librarians have all turned into flesh-eating zombies and are chasing everyone around the library saying 'Brains! Brains!'?

Zoe: Nope. Guess again.

By now I was starting to get a bit twitchy from all that guessing so I said to Zoe, 'I give up, just tell me.'

And Zoe said there was going to be a new art and craft class called Krafty Kids Klub at the library tomorrow morning at 10 o'clock. And she'd signed us both up to be Krafty Kids.

And I said to Zoe, 'Are you JOKING?? You've signed us up for something called Krafty Kids Klub? What if I don't want to be a Krafty Kid? What if the Klub is full of kindy kids with sticky hands doing BABY stuff for BABIES? Bleuchhh.'

And then Zoe agreed the name was **bleuchhh** to the power of 100, but the librarian said that the teacher was **aMAZing**. And that we would all be making **fabulous** craft stuff, which would be **PERFECT** for Christmas presents. (Which reminded me there are still a few people I need to get Christmas presents for.)

I looked out at the sky and it was **STILL RAINING**. What if it was raining again tomorrow? And the tomorrow after that? And for the **WHOLE REST OF THE TOMORROWS OF OUR CHRISTMAS BEACH HOLIDAY?!!!**

And then I thought about all these long, sad, gloomerous, desolate rainy days stretching endlessly ahead of me, where I had to sit in a leaky, creaky caravan playing ancient ~~bored~~ board games with my boring family.

So instead of getting into a big snoot with Zoe about signing me up for the Krafty Kids Klub WITHOUT MY PERMISSION, I said, 'Oh good, thanks, Zoe, you're the best, I can't wait.'

G'night, Diary.

PS Here's a poem I wrote about rain, in between playing exciting games of Go Fish and Snap.

Rain, rain
Go away
You make all the skies
Go grey
Rain, rain
You're a pain
We want sun and fun
Again
So SHOOOOOOOO!

Friday, after dinner

Dear Diary,

There is just so much to tell you, I don't know where to start. So I'll do what my lovely teacher Ms Weiss always says we should do when we're writing a report:

'Begin at the beginning and keep going until you get to the end.'

WARNING: Some of this next bit might be a bit distressing. You have been warned.

I woke up bright and early thinking maybe today will be a lovely **summery, sunful** day after all, and we can forget Krafty Kids Klub ever existed and go to the beach and do normal everyday beach stuff, like watching crabs in the rock pools or burying Olivia up to her neck in sand so she can't try to follow us everywhere and listen in to our secret conversations **EVERY MINUTE OF THE DAY**.

But no. It was not lovely and sunful. It was raining and gloomerous.

So I put on my raincoat and then Mum's raincoat, in case mine leaked, and then Dad's raincoat over the top of that in case Mum's leaked, and got ready to go to Kiddyland Krafty Kids Klub with Zoe.

I was just walking out the door when Mum called me back and said that Olivia wanted to come too. She had that look on her face that mums sometimes get which says there is absolutely NO POINT in arguing with them because you will NEVER WIN. Not even if you use all your S.P.O.P.*

* S.P.O.P. stands for Secret Powers of Persuasion, like offering to do extra jobs around the house or doing something you normally wouldn't ever do, like letting your annoying little sister borrow your stuff. Especially your best glitter pens.

Other people can use it too just by putting the first initial of their name at the front. So mine is E.S.P.O.P. and Zoe's is Z.S.P.O.P.

Sometimes life is so EXASPERATERING, Diary!

Not only did I have to go to a craft class that was (probably) full of little kids making stuff out of toilet-paper rolls,

and colouring outside the edges

and flicking paint at each other,

I had to take Olivia with me as well.

WAAAAAAAAAAHHHHHHHHH!

But that wasn't the **WORSEREST** thing to happen to me today.

There were lots of much more ~~badder~~ worse things than that.

Firstly, we were late.

REASONS WHY WE WERE LATE

1. Olivia was still eating her breakfast when she said she wanted to come too, so I had to sit there staring **huffily** out the window while I waited for her to finish.

2. Olivia kept changing her mind about what she was going to wear.

3 We were finally on our way (with Zoe) when Olivia said she had to run back to our caravan because she'd forgotten something. And then on the way she slipped over in the slippery wet grass. And cut her finger on a bit of tin. (Probably the same bit of tin that made Jimmy Pappas's foot turn black and nearly get cut off. Eww.) And then Bob ran out and tried to lick it better. (Her finger, not the bit of tin.) And then Zoe and I had to stand there waiting while Mum put a bandaid on it. In the rain. We will probably both get ~~new moanya newmonia~~ a nasty disease that makes your lungs fall off.

4 While we were walking to the library Olivia kept complaining in this really whiny voice that her raincoat was leaking so we had to stop **AGAIN** so I could take off one of my raincoats and give it to her before all that whining made my head explode.

5 My head exploded.**

** This didn't actually happen but it could have.

So anyway, by the time we **FINALLY** arrived at the library, Krafty Kids Klub had already started.

The good news

It wasn't **ALL** kindy-aged kids. There were a few other kids there the same age as Zoe and me.

The bad, so Horrifyingly Horrible I almost can't write it down, news

You are not going t

Friday night, a bit later

Sorry, Diary,

Some boys were playing soccer in the dark outside our caravan and they tripped over our electricity cable and it came out of its socket and all the power went off.

Everyone SCREAMED!

Especially Dad and Olivia.

But then Mum went outside and fixed the cable and the light went back on, so now I can go back to telling you about the HH* thing.

* HH = Horrifyingly Horrible.

So, there we were—me, Zoe and Olivia—standing in the doorway in a giganterous puddle made by the rivers of water running off our raincoats. All the other kids were sitting at tables busily making snow domes out of old jam jars and little plastic Christmas trees and snowmen and mountains of glitter.

Olivia pointed to one of the tables and said, 'Look, Ella, aren't they your friends, Jessie and Ana?'

And then Jessie and Ana looked up right at that moment and saw us standing in the doorway looking like **drowned meerkats**.

And guess who was sitting between them, with a big **sneery smirk** all over her **smirky sneery face?**

NOOOOOOOOOOOOOOOOOOOOOOOOO!

My theory about the 7.29 billion people must have been wrong. Peach **is** in Moonlight Bay. ☹

And if she's sitting with Jessie and Ana, that means she must be that 'nice, funny girl' staying at the big new resort with the swimming pool and drinks with little umbrellas in them who Ana said I WOULD LOVE.

There is **NO WAY** in the whole wild world I am **EVER** going to love Perfect Princess Peach Parker. Even if you offered to give me a lifetime voucher for triple-decker choc peanut fudge gelato from the Gelato Shop, any time I wanted, I **STILL** couldn't do it.**

** Though I must admit an offer like that would be **EXTREMELY** temptifying.

And then this weird lady with a calm smile and little plaits all over her head (and the most UN-stylish outfit I have **EVER** seen in my **ENTIRE LIFE**) came over to us. She told us her name was Andromeda Moonbeam

and then she said, 'Quickly, girls, take off those wet raincoats before you catch ~~new~~ ~~moanya~~ ~~newmonia~~ (you know the word I mean) and come and sit down at this nice table here.' And then she pointed to an empty table that was RIGHT BESIDE Jessie and Ana and (that girl). So then THEY all started nudging each other and rolling their eyes and doing pretending-to-be-sick movements, only behind their hands so the calmly-smiling lady couldn't see them.

So I whispered to Zoe, 'Let's just leave right now.' And Zoe whispered back, 'You bet, I'm out of here.'

But then Olivia said in this really loud whiny voice that **EVERYONE** in the room (and probably the room next door) could hear, 'But you **PROMISED** I could come with you to Krafty Kids Klub and if you don't stay I'm going to tell Mum!'

Sometimes Olivia is so annoying she makes my **Head SPIN!!!**

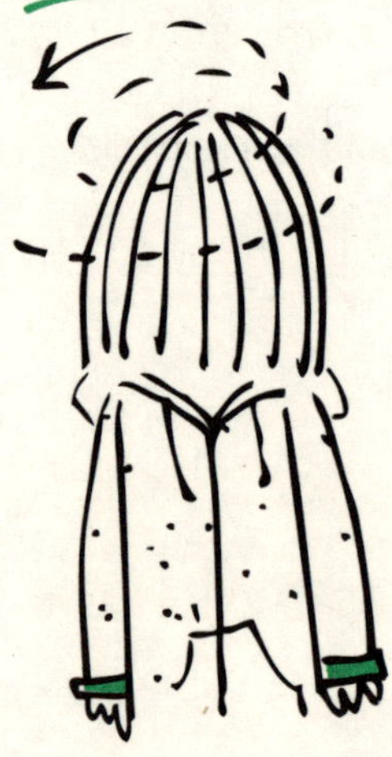

And then I thought about having to trudge through puddles all the way back to the caravan again in the leaky raincoats, past ~~danj~~ dangerous pieces of tin. And what Mum would say to me when we got there.

And then I thought, making cute little snow domes out of jam jars and glitter actually looks kind of fun. Plus a snow dome would make an EXCELLENT Christmas present for Nanna Kate.

So I agreed to stay. On ~~one~~ two conditions:

1. That we could find another table to sit at that was **NOT** next to my ex-BFF and ex-SBFFs.

2. Olivia had to promise **cross her heart hope to die** to keep quiet and not be annoying or even **THINK** about being noisy or annoying.

Fortunately we were able to find a very small table behind some cupboards.

Unfortunately there was already someone sitting at it. A boy called Eduardo, who had an extremely bad sniffing problem. Eww. But at least we were a LONG way away from YKW.***

*** YKW = You Know Who

Andromeda Moonglow came back over and gave us a sheet of rainbow-coloured paper with printed instructions on it for how to make a snow dome. It looked easy-peasy.

Except by the time we got to the Supplies Table to pick up our supplies, there was hardly anything left. All the other Krafty Kids had grabbed the best stuff. Olivia looked like she was about to start blubbing again so I let her have the last little plastic Christmas tree.

And then when Andromeda Starbright wasn't looking, Zoe and I raided the Supplies Cupboard and found a box of cool-looking plastic dinosaurs. So we decided to use a couple of those for our Christmas snow dome scenes instead.

DINOSAURS in the SNOW. ZOW-EE!

The next thing I needed to get for our snow domes was my most favouritest ~~kraft~~ craft product of all time. Glitter!

There was a big jar of it on the Supplies Table. I was carefully ladling enough glitter for me and Zoe and Olivia out of the jar and into a plastic cup when *someone* accidentally on purpose bumped my arm as she walked past.

up

up

Glitter fluttered up into the air and swirled around swirlingly.

It was just like being inside a giganterous snow dome!

And then everyone started sneezing. Especially Eduardo.

'Oopsies!' whispered Peach, right into my ear. Her eyes glittered evilously, like an evilous cat just before it pounces on a sweet little mouse. Then she kept walking right on past, like nothing had even happened.

I sneaked a look over at Jessie and Ana and they were secretly giving her big thumbs-up signs. But before I could say anything, Andromeda Starwalker came running over with a broom and dustpan and said, 'Oh dear, looks like we have a Klumsy Klogs in our Klass!' and then all the other Krafty Kids started laughing and pointing at me and singing, 'Klumsy Klogs, Klumsy Klogs.'

Which was really mean and hurtifying, because it **WASN'T EVEN MY FAULT.**

It's so not fair, Diary. It doesn't matter where I go. Peach Parker will always be there to **RUIN MY LIFE.**

Yours, in desperating desperation,
Ella

☹☹☹☹☹☹☹☹☹☹☹☹☹☹☹☹☹☹☹☹☹☹☹

Saturday morning

Still raining.

Saturday, before lunch

Still raining.

Saturday, after lunch

Still raining.

Mum and Dad and Olivia and Max have all gone to the Kids Komedy Kapers Klub at the library. They're going to watch funny cartoons and movies and eat buckets of tasty, mouth-watering, scrumptious hot buttery popcorn. I LOVE popcorn. But no way am I ever going back to that library ever again. Ever. I am too distraught. So distraught that even if you rounded up a whole herd of wild ~~horses~~ unicorns, with silvery manes and ~~tales~~ tails, and sparkly hooves, and ordered them to drag me there, I STILL wouldn't go.

I'm going to stay up here on my cosy bunk with Bob (and some yummy treats that Mum thoughtfully provided) and write some lovely **artistical** and **heartfelt** poems for everyone's Christmas cards instead.

Love,
Ella xoxo

Christmas greetings
Nanna K8
Everything you do
Is Gr8!
XOX
To my best friend
Hope our friendship
Never ends!

This one Needs a BIT more WORK

Monday night

Dear Diary,

Guess what? It finally STOPPED RAINING!!!

Dad got to go fishing with his mates, Wally and Davo, on their boat. Max and Olivia went too. Mum said she couldn't go because she had some 'special errands'* to run.

* Running 'special errands' is what mums tell their families they are doing when anyone with even a tiny brain knows they are actually going to a big shopping centre to get their hair done or have green goo rubbed all over their face by a lady with purple fingernails. Bleuchhh.

I didn't want to go fishing because:

1 I don't like doing anything that means you have to see dead things or touch slimy things like worms. Eww.

2 I needed to have another Emergency Meeting with Zoe.

So I stayed behind with Zoe and Zoe's mum and Bob and we all (but mainly Bob) ate toasted tinned sardine and peanut butter sandwiches for lunch.**

** Zoe's mum has VERY ~~pakoolyar~~ ~~perkulier~~ original ideas about food combinations. Which is why Zoe likes to spend A LOT of time at my place.

After that, we took Bob for a nice relaxing walk to the Moonlight Bay Op Shop to see if we could find some winning outfits for the Christmas Eve Fancy Dress Parade.

Unfortunately for Bob the ~~ainsh~~ ancient ladies who work in the Op Shop wouldn't let him come in to try anything on. So he had to wait outside while we rummaged happily through the Bargain Bin for Bargains.

I was just picking out a sweet little knitted hat with red pom poms on it which was **PERFECT** for our Christmas theme when the doorbell tinkled and three girls came into the shop.

And guess who it was?

Ka-ching! You win.

Princess Peach and my ex-SBFFs. They were all wearing matching outfits. Even their hairstyles were matching.

I immediately went into ninja ~~kammaflarge~~ camouflage mode and squeezed behind a flowery curtain that was EXACTLY the same colour as my outfit.

From there I sent a series of complicated hand signals to Zoe telling her to duck down behind the rack of assorted men's pants so Peach and her new best friends couldn't see her either.

Then we set our ears to ultrasonic listening-in mode so we could listen in.

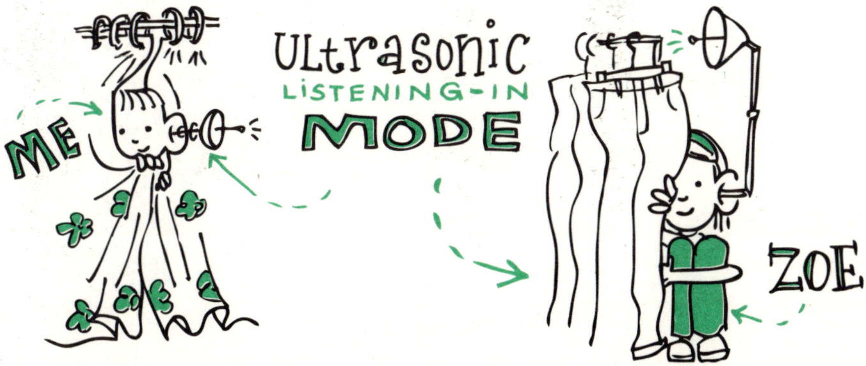

This is what we heard:

Peach (rummaging noises): Oooo. Look at this sweet little dress. It would look so aDORable on darling Mitzi.

Zoe and me (mouthing to each other): *Mitzi??????*

Jessie and Ana (nodding and speaking together at the same time): **aDORable.**

Peach: Oh, but look, it's pink. Jessie? Go and ask the lady if it comes in red. Or green. Or red and green.

Jessie (puzzled): Huh?

Jessie

Peach (rolling her eyes): You know, Christmas colours? For the Christmas Eve Fancy Dress Parade for Pets and their Owners? You want us to **WIN**, don't you?

Jessie (even more puzzled): But op shops don't have—

I never got to find out what op shops don't have because right at that very exact same moment the doorbell tinkled **AGAIN** and even **MORE** people came in. And they started heading straight for the assorted men's pants rack.

NOOOOOOOOOOOOOOO!

I had to get Zoe out of there. Fast.

I quickly sent a complicated series of advanced hand signals to Zoe to describe what she had to do. Then we got down on the floor on our hands and knees and crept from rack to rack, ninja-style, until we reached the front door and slipped back out into the street.

I untied Bob and we quickly jogged to a nice safe-looking bench in the park around the corner so we could have an emergency Emergency Meeting.

This is what we said:

Me: I am **SHOCKED!**

Zoe: Same.

Me: How come Peach ALWAYS has to copy everything I do? Now she's going to enter the **EXACT SAME** competition as us. Just so she can beat me. Again.

Zoe: It's so not fair.

Me: But *WHY? WHY* is she entering the section for Pets and their Owners?

Peach doesn't even have a pet. Especially one called Mitzi.

Zoe: What are you going to do about it?

Me: I don't know yet. **SOMEthing**. But first we need to collect **MORE INFORMATION**.

We sat there on the bench in the summery sun for a while. Then I took out my notebook and pencil which I always keep handy in case I need to jot something down, and started jotting down the extra things we needed to know.

EXTRA THINGS WE NEED TO KNOW

1. Who or what is Mitzi?
2. If Mitzi is a dog (most likely), what ~~bread~~ breed is she?
3. And where does she come from?

4. And how did Peach get her?
5. And why does Peach always have to be so mean?

Sometimes life is extremely complicatifying, Diary. I am amazed anybody ever gets anything done.

Tuesday evening

Ho, ho, ho, Diary,

It is Christmas Eve Eve!*

* which, if you only have a VERY tiny brain, means the day BEFORE Christmas Eve.

Everyone in Moonlight Gardens is starting to get very exciterated.

There is a **giganterous** Christmas tree outside the manager's office with lots of **shiny dingly dangly** things hanging off it and a sweet little Christmas ~~angle~~ angel on the top.

And all the holiday people have been decorating their vans and practising their carols for the Carols by Candlelight concert on the beach tonight and inviting their neighbours over for special Christmas drinks and snacks.

Our family spent practically **THE WHOLE DAY** wrapping up presents for each other (which is **EXTREMELY** hard to do when you have **NO** ~~privercy~~ privacy) so we had to take it in turns.

Here's what I got for everyone (using my dog-walking money):

Mum: Her favourite smelly hand lotion and bath salts

Dad: A mug that says **BEST DAD IN THE WORLD** that I made in art class at school

Olivia: Her very own set of glitter pens (so she doesn't have to keep borrowing mine all the time)

Max: A pirate eye-patch

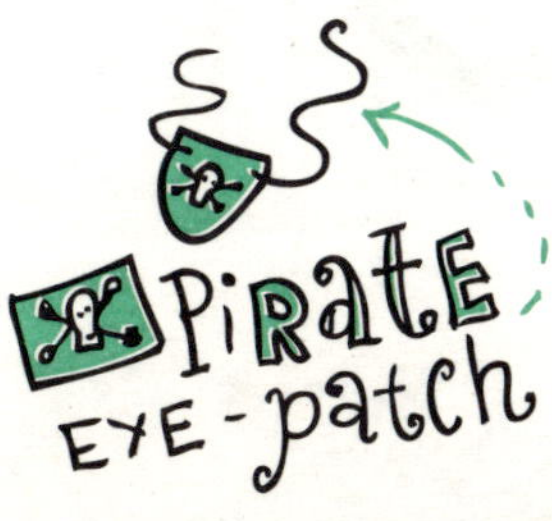

Bob: A bouncy ball I found on the beach (it was only slightly chewed)

Nanna Kate: My dinosaur snow dome from Krafty Kids Klub

Zoe: A secret ~~privet~~ private diary just like mine, where she can write all her own secret private secrets. I hope she likes it!

Then we decorated our caravan walls with tinsel and plastic holly that Mum got on special at the Moonlight Bay Bargain Mart.

There was just enough left over for Zoe and me to add to the exceptionally excellent Christmas-themed outfit we're making for Bob.

BOB'S CHRISTMAS-THEMED OUTFIT FOR THE CHRISTMAS EVE PARADE

Max was really worried that Santa won't be able to find him in our caravan to give him his presents. And also that there will be nowhere for his reindeer to park.

And then Mum told him everything would be OK because Santa has a special map that shows where EVERYONE in the world is on Christmas Eve, even if it was the bottom bunk of a leaky, creaky caravan in Moonlight Bay.

Max is HERE!

ZZZ
ZZZZZZ

And Dad told him he'd made **Special Arrangements** with the manager of the caravan park to allow the reindeer to park on top of the shower block. Which is why it is always a bit smelly. ☺

WARNING

DAD JOKE

And then Max stopped being worried and we all went to the beach and played beach cricket and I had so much fun I forgot all about mean old Peach Parker and Jessie and Ana and the mysterious Mitzi mystery. (For a little while, anyway.)

I can't wait for tomorrow!

Merry Christmas Eve Eve, Diary.

Love,

Ella xoxo

Wednesday night, very, very late

Dear Diary,

There is SO much to tell you! So I'll just skip the bits like what we ate for lunch and the rude word* Olivia said to me when I accidentally smashed her My Little Bunny mug, and tell you the most interesting, excitering parts, like what happened at the Moonlight Bay Christmas Eve Party and Fancy Dress Parade.

* It wasn't even that rude, Diary. Zoe knows MUCH ruder words than that.

Sunset Park was full of people and their pets wearing matching Christmas outfits, waiting for the contest to start. We even saw a girl with a darling little Christmas bunny on a lead!

WHAT ZOE, ME AND BOB WERE WEARING

Zoe and me and Bob all looked aMAZing, of course, in our matching outfits. I spent **HOURS** making sure we would be the most **super-stylish** contestants in the contest.

We were just rehearsing our winners' speeches when . . .

Da da da . . . DUM.

Guess who turned up, parading around in a fancy outfit like a movie star out of a movie?

Princess Smartyface Peach Parker. with a dog on a sparkly lead. Ha!

WHAT PRINCESS PEACH AND HER DOG WERE WEARING

Jessie and Ana were walking right behind Peach and Mitzi, handing out fancy schmancy brochures about a place called the Grande Royale Regal Resort and Spa.

And guess what?!

You never will and there's still lots more to write about so I'll just tell you.

The letters on Mitzi's fur cape matched the name of the resort!

So now I had the answers to Queries 1 – 4 from my list of **EXTRA THINGS WE NEED TO KNOW**.

1. Who or what is Mitzi? A dog

2. If Mitzi is a dog (most likely), what ~~bread~~ breed is she? Italian greyhound

3. And where does she come from? The big new posh resort where Peach is staying!!!

4. And how did Peach get her? Peach must have borrowed her from the owners of the resort so she could go in the contest and beat me and RUIN MY LIFE AGAIN!!!

And then before I could work out the answer to Query 5, a big stripy dog ran up and snatched Mitzi's shiny Christmas baubles in its giganterous teeth and tried to run away with them.

But Mitzi pulled back really hard so it couldn't take them.

And then the stripy dog pulled back even harderer. And they had a giganterous tug of war!

Then the stripy dog let go all of a sudden and Mitzi fell backwards and crashed into the judges' table and all the trophies for the Dog Parade contest fell off and smashed.

And Mitzi got a fright and ran away and no-one could find her.

Now Peach is in BIG TROUBLE with the dog's owners AND everyone else in Moonlight Bay because they had to cancel the parade. And so are Jessie and Ana. Ha!

Good night, Diary. Only one more sleep till Christmas Day!

PS I *do* hope they find dear little Mitzi soon. It is extremely tragical to think that she might be curled up under a prickly bush or lying in a deep hole somewhere, lost and lonely and frighterened. ☹

Wednesday morning, very, very early, so early even Santa hasn't been yet

I just had the most terrible dream!

In my dream I was at the beach, swimming joyfully in a giant rock pool with little fish tickling my toes.

And then the sky went all black and darkerous. And giganterous waves were bashing and crashing over giganterous rocks. And then I noticed a teeny tiny animal with white fur, shivering shiveringly at the very top of the toppest rock.

And then . . .

OOOOO!
I THINK I KNOW WHERE MITZI IS!!!

Have to go now, Diary. Before it's too late!

Wednesday, a bit later

Guess what! I was right!

You know those rock pools, where Zoe and I did our scientifical research? Well, that's where Mitzi was, just like in my dream! In a little cave, at the top of all the rocks!

That's where she ran away to last night.

And then when the tide came in, she got trapped there.

And Zoe and I (and Dad and Mum and Zoe's mum, after I woke them all up) found her and saved her. All because of my dream! I must have secretly known in the deepest part of my brain, because that's where I'd go too if I was frightened or sad.

And Fred and Leila (the owners of Mitzi and GRRRS) are going to give me an extra-special special reward for finding her!

Sorry, Diary, have to go. I just remembered it's Christmas Day, which means I have lots of VIPs (Very Important Presents) to open!!!

Merry Christmas!

Love,

Ella xoxoxoxoxox

PS (one day later)

Jessie and Ana came over to wish me a Merry Christmas and to say they were really, really sorry for being so mean to me, **ESPECIALLY** since I'd always been such a good friend to them. And then they said they hoped I was coming back to Moonlight Gardens next year so we could all have fun together again.

And then we all went for a swim (Zoe came too) and linked pinkies in the waves and made NEW SBFF wishes.

Bet you'll NEVER guess what I wished for! ☺

PPS (two days later)

Bet you're dying to find out what my extra-special special reward was!

Fred and Leila invited Zoe and me to have lunch at GRRRS.

It was **fantabulously fabulous!**

We lounged around the pool on long chairs and ate posh hamburgers and chips and a man brought us drinks on a tray, with little umbrellas in them, just like the ones Jessie and Ana had.

And guess what! The man said we could have **anything** we wanted for dessert. **ANYTHING!**

Guess what I chose? ☺☺☺

And guess what else? While we were sitting there, Peach and her mum walked past. They were both eating **triple-decker ice-creams** too.

Peach was looking the other way, trying her hardest not to notice me.

So she didn't see the beach ball come flying out of the pool until it hit her on the arm, which knocked her ice-cream out of her hand, and ALL OVER her lacy white top and shorts.

Oopsies!

ELLA Diaries

Read more of Ella's brilliant diary in

Double Dare You

Ballet Backflip

I ♥ Pets

Dreams come true

Pony School Showdown

and look out for more coming soon!